THE ANGEL GABRIEL COMES TO MARY

NAME _______________________________

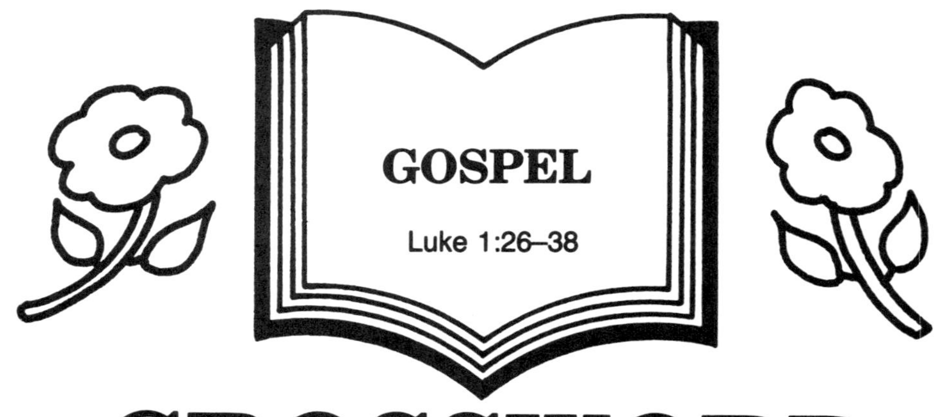

CROSSWORD PUZZLE

In the Gospel reading, Mary has a special visitor. Put the words from the story into the crossword puzzle. (If you need help, use the word list.)

God sent the (*1 down*) Gabriel to Mary. Gabriel said, "Do not be (*1 across*), Mary." He said she would have a (*2 across*). She should call Him (*3 across*). "How will this be?" Mary (*4 down*). Gabriel said the baby would be the Son of (*5 down*). "I am the Lord's (*6 across*)," said Mary.

WORD LIST:

ASKED
GOD
JESUS
AFRAID
SERVANT
ANGEL
SON

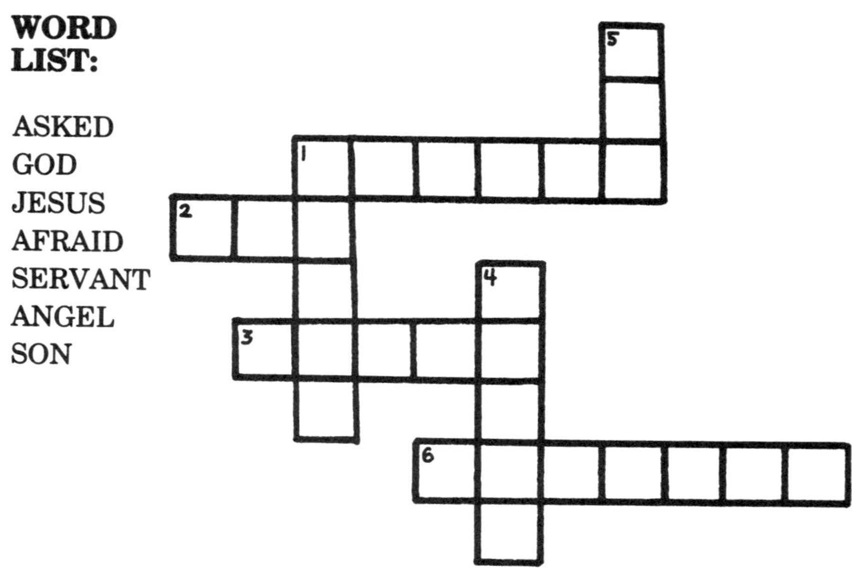

HIDDEN MESSAGE

The angel said many important things to Mary. Circle every third letter in the puzzle and write them on the lines below. Then divide them into words to learn one of those important things.

SOMETHING TO DRAW
How do you think Mary looked . . .
when she saw the angel?
when she heard what he said?
after he left?
CROSSWORD PUZZLE:
SERVANT
ASKS
JESUS
SONG
AFRAID
GOD
ANSWERS
HIDDEN MESSAGE:
For nothing is impossible with God.
© 1988, 1993 CPH
Printed in U.S.A.

MARY VISITS ELIZABETH

NAME ___________________________

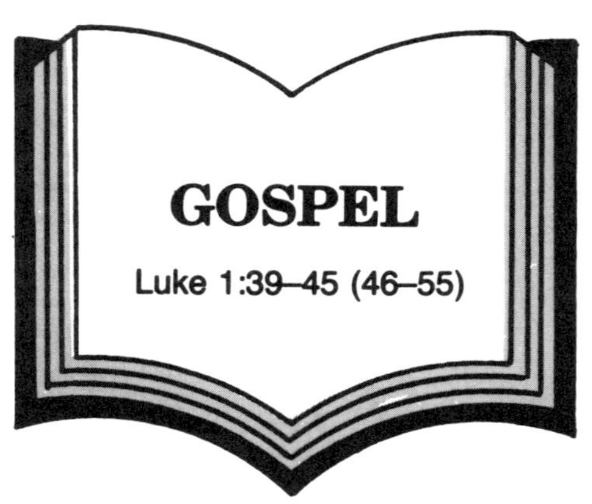

HIDDEN MESSAGE

In the Gospel reading, Elizabeth was very glad to see Mary. Circle every third letter in the puzzle and write them on the lines below. Then divide them into words to learn one thing Elizabeth said.

```
T A B U A L E T
E R A S B A S T
G E R A D M A I
C A S S E T R A
H O N E B A C K
S H I N I E R L
D A D A N Y G O
O W L U D A W N
B I G E L O A L
T A B B R E A N
A K A R
```

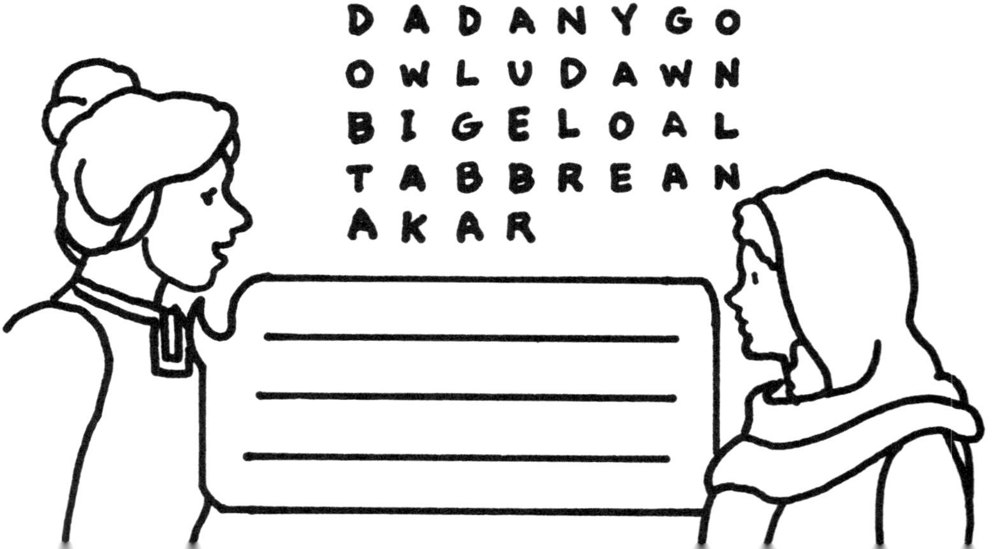

A MAZE
Help Mary find her way
to Elizabeth's house.

SOMETHING TO DRAW

Printed in U.S.A.

JOSEPH HAS A DREAM

NAME ________________________

HIDDEN MESSAGE

In the Gospel, the angel tells Joseph some important things. Circle every third letter in the puzzle and write them on the lines below. Then divide them into words to find out one of the important things.

EMPTY SQUARES

The angel also told Joseph something important about Jesus. See if you can fit those words into the squares below. One word has been done for you.

HE WILL SAVE HIS PEOPLE FROM THEIR SINS.

HIDDEN PICTURE

The angel told Joseph about a special baby. Color the spaces with dots to find out that baby's name.

SOMETHING TO DRAW

Use the space below to draw a picture of an angel.

ANSWERS

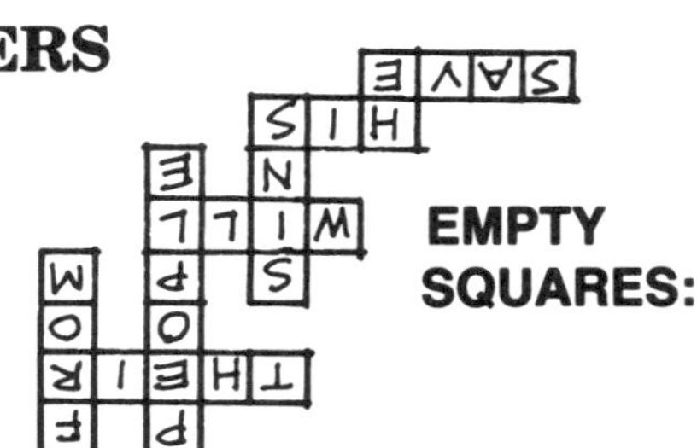

HIDDEN MESSAGE:
She will give birth
to a son.

HIDDEN PICTURE:
Jesus

**EMPTY
SQUARES:**

JESUS IS BORN IN BETHLEHEM

NAME ___________________________

WORD SEARCH

Try to find ten words from the Gospel story in this puzzle. You may go up or down, from side to side, or diagonally. Circle each word as you find it and mark it off the list. The first one has been done for you.

JOSEPH
MARY
MANGER
INN
SHEPHERD
FLOCKS
ANGEL
GLORY
PEACE
SAVIOR

SOMETHING TO DRAW

Imagine how everyone felt that first Christmas! Draw in their faces below.

DOT-TO-DOT

This animal saw angels on the first Christmas. Connect the dots to see what it is.

THE ANGELS TELL THE SHEPHERDS

NAME ________________________

HIDDEN WORD

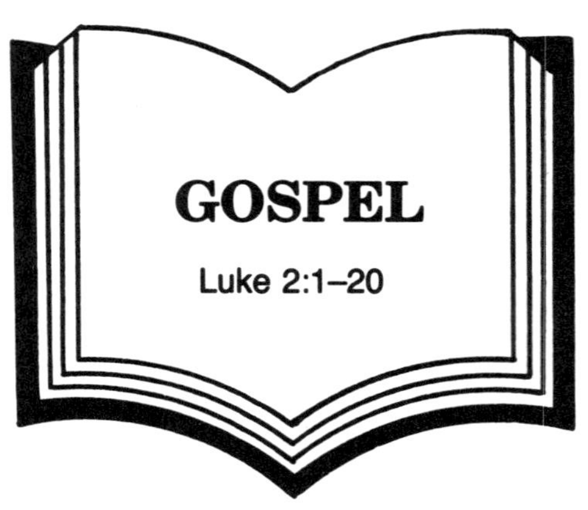

To find out what the angels sang in the Gospel reading, color the spaces with dots.

SOMETHING TO DRAW

SOMETHING ELSE TO DRAW

In the space below, draw your own picture of the first Christmas.

SIMEON PRAISES GOD

NAME _______________________________

GOSPEL
Luke 2:25–40
A MAZE
Find the way Simeon went from his house to the temple in Jerusalem.

WORD SEARCH

Try to find 12 words from the Gospel story in this puzzle. You may go up or down, from side to side, or diagonally. Circle each word as you find it and mark it off the list. The first one has been done for you.

SIMEON	CHILD	GLORY	OLD
SPIRIT	PEACE	SIGN	THANKS
TEMPLE	EYES	ANNA	GRACE

DOT-TO-DOT

Anna and Simeon were very excited and happy. Connect the dots to see who made them feel that way.

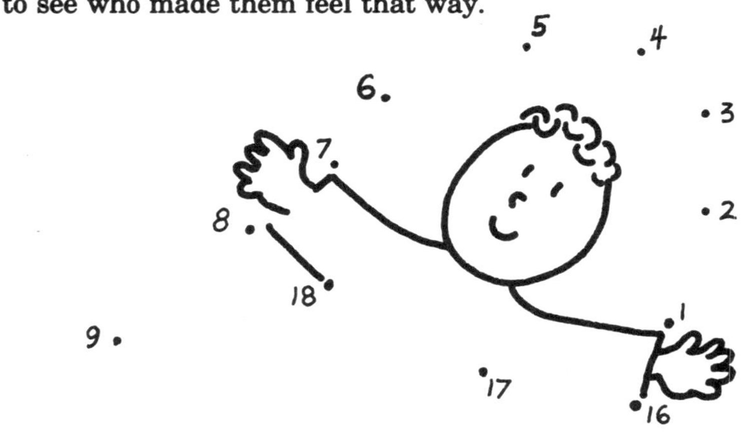

ANSWERS

WORD SEARCH:

Printed in U.S.A.

THE WISE MEN WORSHIP JESUS

NAME ___________________

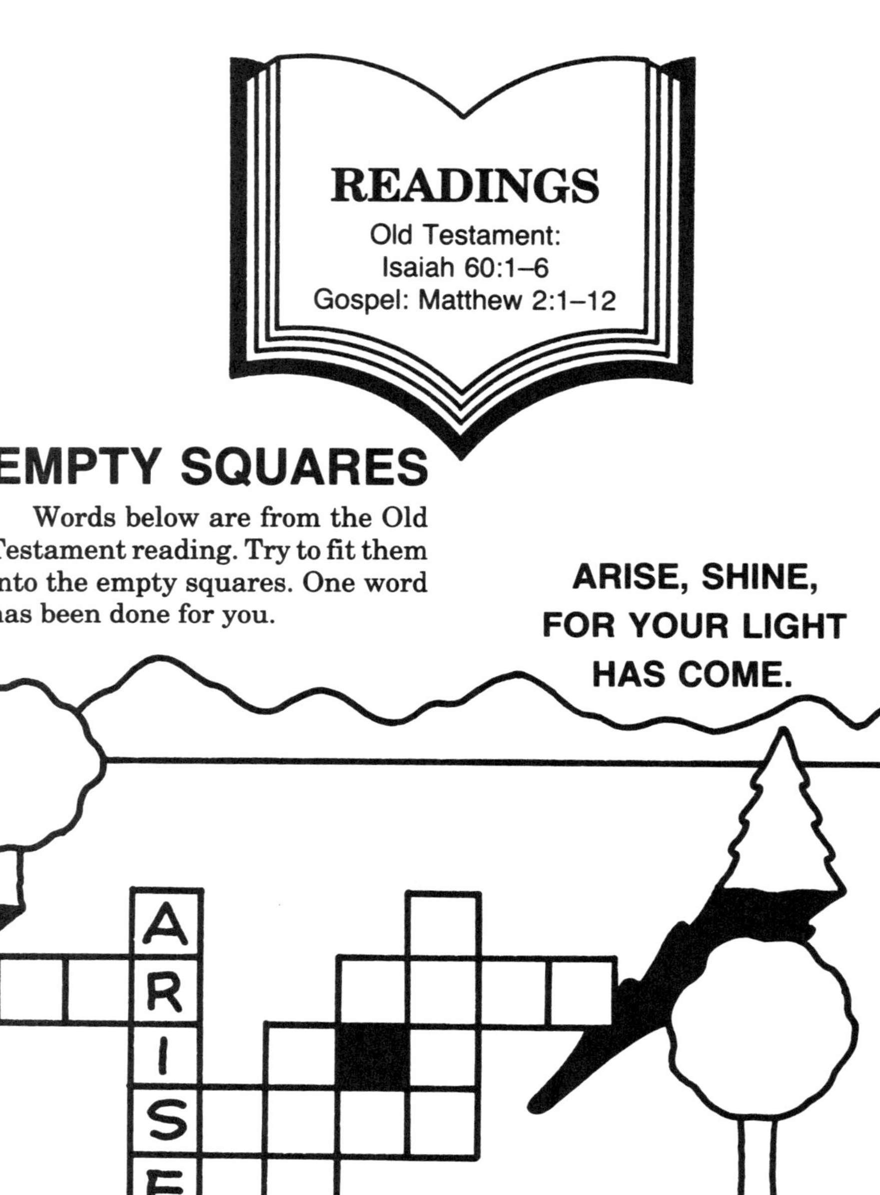

EMPTY SQUARES

Words below are from the Old Testament reading. Try to fit them into the empty squares. One word has been done for you.

A MAZE

Can you help the Wise Men
follow the star to Bethlehem?

DOT-TO-DOT

Many people think the Wise Men rode animals like this. Connect the dots to see what it is.

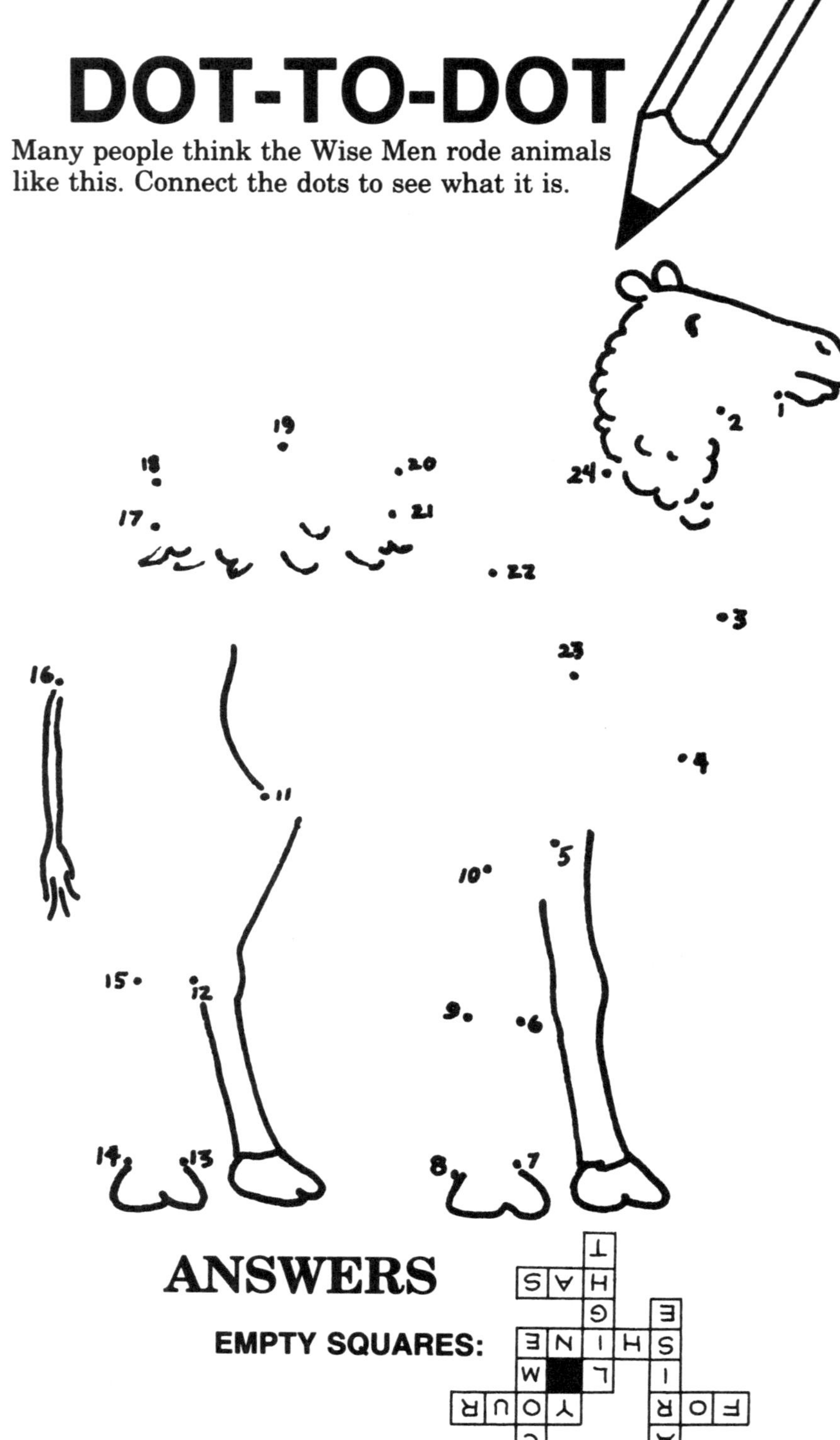

ANSWERS

EMPTY SQUARES:

THE ESCAPE TO EGYPT

NAME _______________________________

SCRAMBLED WORDS

Unscramble these words from the Gospel story. Print them on the lines on the right side. Then print the circled letters on the line below. They will tell you who talked to Joseph.

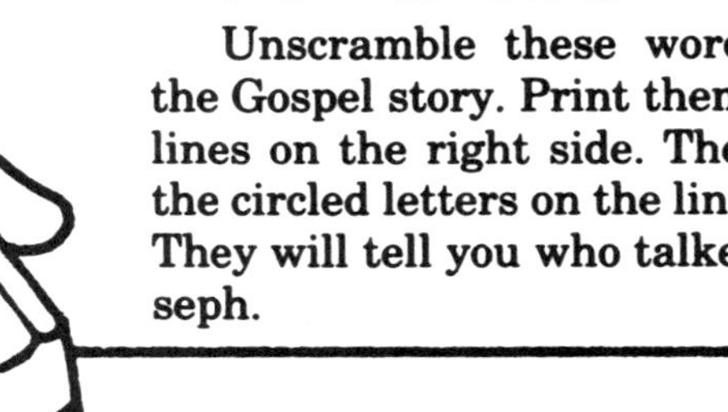

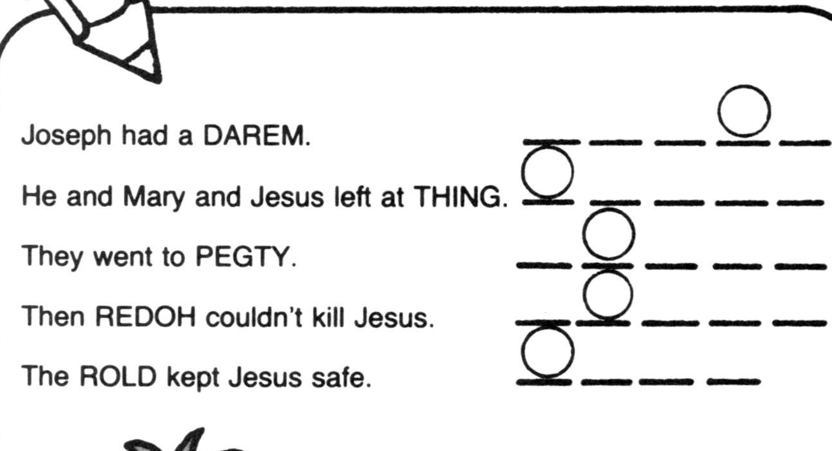

Joseph had a DAREM.

He and Mary and Jesus left at THING.

They went to PEGTY.

Then REDOH couldn't kill Jesus.

The ROLD kept Jesus safe.

A MAZE
Color in the circles that will take Jesus and His family to Egypt.

CODE MESSAGE

Long ago the prophets said something about Jesus. In the Gospel reading it comes true. To find out what they said, you must write the correct letter under each number. The key will tell you which letter to write.

8 5   23 9 12 12   2 5   3 1 12 12 5 4

___ ___   ___ ___ ___ ___   ___ ___   ___ ___ ___ ___ ___ ___

1   14 1 26 1 18 5 14 5

___   ___ ___ ___ ___ ___ ___ ___ ___ .

KEY

1 = A	8 = H	15 = O	22 = V
2 = B	9 = I	16 = P	23 = W
3 = C	10 = J	17 = Q	24 = X
4 = D	11 = K	18 = R	25 = Y
5 = E	12 = L	19 = S	26 = Z
6 = F	13 = M	20 = T	
7 = G	14 = N	21 = U	

ANSWERS

SCRAMBLED WORDS: dream, night, Egypt, Herod, Lord—angel

CODE MESSAGE: He will be called a Nazarene.